Portfolio Development for Paraeducators

Portfolio Development for Paraeducators

Suzanne Koprowski
Waukesha County Technical College

Carol A. Long
Winona State University

PEARSON

Boston   New York   San Francisco
Mexico City   Montreal   Toronto   London   Madrid   Munich   Paris
Hong Kong   Singapore   Tokyo   Cape Town   Sydney

Executive Series Editor: Virginia Lanigan
Editorial Assistant: Scott Blaszak
Executive Marketing Manager (College): Amy Cronin Jordan
Marketing Manager (Professional): Jennifer Armstrong
Editorial-Production Administrator: Anna Socrates
Manufacturing Buyer: Andrew Turso
Cover Coordinator: Joel Gendron
Composition and Prepress Buyer: Linda Cox
Editorial-Production Service: Susan McNally
Text Design and Electronic Composition: Glenna Collett

For related titles and support materials, visit our online catalogue at www.ablongman.com.

Between the time Web site information is gathered and then published, it is not unusual for some sites to have closed. Also, the transcription of URLs can result in unintended typographical errors. The publisher would appreciate notification where these errors occur so that they may be corrected in subsequent editions.

CIP data not available at time of publication.

ISBN: 0-205-43464-9

Printed in the United States of America
10 9 8 7 6 5 4 3 2 1   10 09 08 07 06 05 04

Dedicated to the paraeducators who so selflessly serve school children, many working under difficult conditions without recognition or adequate compensation. May this book help them to find that acknowledgment and assist them to increase their contribution to the children they serve.

Contents

CHAPTER ONE

What Is a Professional Portfolio?

A portfolio is an organized, unique, and ongoing collection of artifacts to document an individual's knowledge, skills and personal traits that enhance her or his job performance. It is a tangible way to let others know about the knowledge and skills we possess. Paraeducators bring to the classroom, often unknowingly, a wealth of talents, knowledge, and skills. For example, at a portfolio workshop session, a paraeducator was asked what she brought to the classroom, what were her talents, her areas of knowledge, and her skills. She replied, "Well, I don't have any." The three other paraeducators from her district immediately chimed in and listed a dozen ways she contributed.

She responded with "Oh yes, that's right, but I didn't want to brag." A portfolio provides a means to demonstrate in a realistic, positive, professional manner, without bragging, what we bring to the classroom. It is a way to gain recognition that is rightly deserved.

A portfolio is an excellent arena for displaying a range of skills, perhaps from organizational ability to sign language proficiency, or from touch math knowledge to computer literacy. To be a paraeducator in today's schools means much more than clerical duties and supervising the playground. Today's paraeducators utilize highly skilled procedures such as tube feeding, assisting with children who have emotional disorders and are self-injurious, reinforcing math and reading skills, using specialized instructional techniques, and working with numerous school and agency personnel with a high level of communication savvy. The knowledge and skills required to work effectively are numerous, diverse, complex,

> Motivation is what gets you started. Habit is what keeps you going.
> —Unknown

and dynamic in the ever changing field of education.

A professional portfolio can be a means by which the paraeducator illustrates the need for additional training, by focusing on what is currently brought to the classroom and comparing that with the specific needs of that situation. From that focus can come future development through professional goals and support for more training specific to personal needs and position.

A final purpose related to portfolio development is to encourage dialogue and collaboration among paraeducators, teachers, and administrators and to act as a catalyst for opening the door for discussion. The portfolio serves as a conversation starter, a means to facilitate interaction by acknowledging where paraeducators are and planning for where they want to go.

Why Is a Professional Portfolio Needed?

Today many professions require individuals to develop a professional portfolio either to acquire or to retain a job. Most teachers are now required to compile a professional portfolio. Since paraeducators are part of the educational team, it logically follows that paraeducators can also learn and benefit from developing their own professional portfolios.

Often paraeducators work with students with the most intense needs, yet receive little, if any, training. Frequently the training received is too little, too late. A portfolio documents the training already received and provides the basis for further professional development through a reflective process related to needs identification and personal goal setting.

As a workshop on portfolios for paraeducators progressed, one of the participants moved from skeptical to highly enthusiastic. She said, "I know how I can use this. I can take it to my school board when we go to bargain and prove how valuable I am! I have a lot of special

skills and can work effectively with some of the most challenging students in my school." A professional portfolio is documentation of an employee's worth and the contributions she makes to the classroom and the education of students, at the same time substantiating a need for additional training. Too often, supervisors or administrators are just not fully aware of the breadth of the paraeducator impact on the success of the educational program and the students supported through that program. The portfolio is a tool to use when justifying a position and/or seeking advancement. It is a means to demonstrate impact and competence in the classroom in a concrete fashion.

As one paraeducator with more than twenty years of experience was compiling her portfolio she said, "This is the best thing I've ever done! I have learned so much about myself and what I bring to my job. I knew I was good and now I know why!"

Perhaps the most important reason for developing a portfolio is the personal satisfaction it provides. The portfolio process is reflective. It requires thought and insight into both the personal self and the position. It documents where employees are and provides direction for where they can go. The process is a celebration of achievement and growth; and the portfolio itself is a personal record of professional development and accomplishments, qualified artifacts, and reflective works.

What Are the Different Types of Professional Portfolios?

There are two basic types of portfolios used in education:

- Interview/Presentation
- Professional Development/Process

The interview portfolio is designed to help acquire a desired position. It contains, among other things, a resume, letters of recommendation, a high school diploma, and comprehensive documentation of any additional training and experience. The professional development portfolio is generally specific to a current job or educational training program, and may contain documentation that relates to the educational program experience or job description, individual student needs, standards, district policies, and professional development goals.

Portfolios for paraeducators who are at various stages in their career will have different items and organizational structures. These career stages can be divided into:

- Prospective students applying for admission to training programs.
- Students, training to become paraeducators.
- Novice paraeducators, who have less than three years of experience.
- Experienced paraeducators, who have been on the job for three or more years.

Several things will be evident when an individual creates a portfolio. First, each portfolio will be unique. No two portfolios are the same. Each reflects the owner's knowledge, skills, and dispositions. Second, to truly reflect the owner, a portfolio development must be ongoing and updated regularly. As employees develop professionally, portfolios should change to adequately reflect that growth. Third, what goes in the portfolio is a personal decision. The portfolio belongs to the owner and only she or he has the final say about the contents. Finally, this process is one of sharing, appreciating, shaping, and celebrating. Growing professionally is a wonderful experience. It makes everyone more effective in the job. It offers a greater opportunity to contribute, to make the world a better place, and to paraeducators it provides great personal satisfaction. By sharing portfolios, paraeductors share their growth and gain appreciation and recognition. Together they celebrate achievements.

This manual has been developed to assist paraeducators on the journey to sharing, appreciating, and celebrating. Answers to the following questions will be presented:

- How do I organize my professional portfolio?
- What goes into my professional portfolio?
- How do I present my professional portfolio?
- How do I update my professional portfolio?
- How do I evaluate my professional portfolio?

- How do I plan for future professional development?
- How do I organize a team to support my professional development?

As the portfolio develops, keep in mind that each portfolio is unique and along the way it may change as experience and knowledge broaden. It may become more inclusive of the role played in the classroom and reflective of your impact. Experiences may help clarify personal beliefs or values. Paraeducators may recognize areas to target for further growth or may realize career changes that need to be made. The one rule for creating a portfolio is that whatever is collected and presented must be practical, reflective, and designed to encourage professional development. The paraeducator must be prepared for tremendous personal and professional growth as progress continues. The reflective process inherent in portfolio development may well lead to new paths to explore. It can be one of the most meaningful experiences of a lifetime!

CHAPTER TWO

Portfolio Development: Phase I

How Does One Begin?

It is never too early, nor too late to tackle the challenge of organizing a personal, professional portfolio, be it an interview/presentation or a professional development/process portfolio. Whether you are just entering the paraeducator field or are an experienced veteran, the time is now. The key to getting started is reflecting upon abilities and experiences, and selectively collecting data or documents that speak of related experiences, acquired skills and knowledge, talents, and training. Using a file box, an accordion file, or even a shoebox, start gathering concrete evidence documenting qualifications now! Several ideas are offered in this workbook for quickly gathering documents and artifacts appropriate for use in the portfolio.

> Leave as little to chance as possible. Preparation is the key to success.
>
> —Paul Brown

Brainstorming: What Are My Strengths?

To get started in the brainstorming mode take some quiet time to self-reflect by considering varied personal and professional qualifications. Which could serve to enhance performance as a paraeducator? Diverge a bit as you engage in brainstorming to comprehensively take a personal inventory of all your varied abilities and experiences, whether directly or indirectly related to the field of education. Too often we overlook personal strengths and talents

3. What related volunteer work have I done?

- ❏ Coaching
- ❏ Scouting
- ❏ Religious Education
- ❏ Parent Teacher Group
- ❏ Room Parent
- ❏ Community Groups
- ❏ Other

4. What educational experiences have I acquired on the job?

➔ Experience working with students with special needs

- ❏ Learning Disabilities
- ❏ Cognitive Disabilities
- ❏ Emotional/Behavioral Disorders
- ❏ Attention Deficit Disorders
- ❏ Autism Spectrum Disorders
- ❏ Visual/Hearing Impairment
- ❏ Physical Handicaps/Seizures
- ❏ Speech/Language Disorders/Communication Difficulties
- ❏ Other

→ Experience working in differing instructional settings

❏ Inclusion Classroom Setting

❏ Resource Room

❏ Computer Lab

❏ Title I Program

❏ Bilingual Program/ESL Support

❏ Alternative School Program or "At Risk" Program

❏ Other

5. What instructional strategies have I acquired through my professional experience? (i.e., specific reading programs, communication systems, math instructional approaches, OT, PT, Speech/Language or Sign Language implementation)

❏ Implementation of Speech/Language Goals

❏ Facilitation of Phonemic Awareness

❏ Facilitation of Guided Reading

❏ Storytelling

❏ Utilization of Specific Reading Programs/Methods: ERE, SRA . . .

❏ Guiding Daily Oral Language

❏ Job Coaching

❏ Computer Tutoring

❏ Other

6. What supervisory experiences have I had?

❑ Lunchroom

❑ Playground

❑ Bus

❑ Computer Lab

❑ Library

❑ Other

7. What communication or leadership strengths do I possess?

❑ Employee Assistance

❑ Peer Mentor

❑ Committee Chairperson

❑ Web Pages Created

❑ Newsletter Involvement

❑ Other

7. List continuing education training:

➜ Workshops, Conferences, Seminars attended (Record in order on the formal record form on page 15.)

➜ Medical Training

❏ CPR Training

❏ Red Cross First Aid

❏ Tube Feeding

❏ Seizure Awareness

❏ Other

CHAPTER THREE

Portfolio Development: Phase II

Gathering Evidence of Skills and Knowledge

Clear, reflective understanding of job-related skills and experience leads to the next phase of portfolio development. Phase II involves decision making regarding the skills or competencies to be illustrated and included within the portfolio and gathering evidence supporting the claims. A well-developed portfolio is characterized by thoughtful, systematic collection of data and materials. Consider a variety of sources for documenting skills and select documentation or artifacts that best reflect or demonstrate those skills. Possible sources of documentation may include the following:

- Professional licenses or diplomas
- Higher education program brochures

- Certificates of training; in-service training
- Conference brochures; certificates of attendance; handouts with written reflection
- Letters: references, recommendations
- Personal notes: notes of appreciation from students and/or parents
- Artifacts such as work samples personally created
- Photographs of learning centers or materials personally prepared
- Photographs of classroom displays personally created
- Written philosophy statement reflecting personal beliefs
- Professional evaluations or feedback forms related to the job or school performance
- Reflection statements

It opportunity doesn't knock, build a door.
—Milton Berle

Professional Development/Continuing Education Record Form, *continued*

Courses/Training Sessions—Titles	Institution/Agency—Dates

CHAPTER FOUR

Portfolio Organization/ Contents: Phase III

How Does One Organize the Portfolio?

The organizational structure and appearance of a portfolio immediately makes a statement about the developer. A neat, logically sequenced portfolio gives the reviewer a glimpse of organizational abilities and attention to detail. It also expresses one's individuality. Certain guidelines can be employed to dramatically enhance the professional appearance and functionality of the portfolio.

> *People want to know how much you care before they care how much you know.*
>
> *—James F. Hind*

Physical Properties

1. **Three-Ring Binder.** Select a quality, three-ring binder that is durable, clean-lined, and very professional in appearance.

While a leather binder looks sleek and businesslike, a quality vinyl binder can look just as nice and costs considerably less. Select a binder with a complete zip closure design. A zip closure will ensure protection of your important documents and keep them from getting wrinkled, torn, or stained. Discount stores and office supply dealers carry a variety of binder options for consideration.

2. **Document Protector Sheets.** To further protect important documents from damage during handling and to keep individual pages neat and clean, invest in clear plastic sheet protectors, enough for each document in your portfolio. Sheet protectors also give the portfolio an organized,

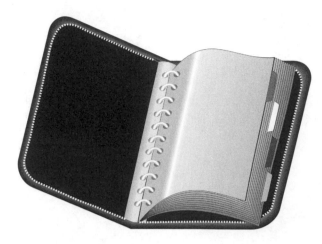

professional look and eliminate the need to punch holes in portfolio documents.

- **Heavy Stock Paper.** As documents are collected over the years, create a fresh, updated look. Copy documents onto a consistent neutral paper. Invest in high quality, heavy stock, plain white or cream-colored business paper. Always keep original documents and photo negatives or duplicates in another storage place for safekeeping. Discount stores or office supply stores carry a variety of professional-looking papers from which to choose, at a very affordable cost.

- **Divider Tabs.** Divider pages with labeled tabs serve to organize documents according to categories. They make referencing desired information quick and efficient during an interview or evaluation meeting. Tabs should be clearly visible when the portfolio is open. As an alternative, colored self-stick index tabs can be affixed directly onto clear sheet protectors and can be used as extenders, if need be.

Portfolio Categories

Depending on the materials or documents collected, determine appropriate categorical sections for organizing data and artifacts.

Included in this manual is a portfolio checklist, which provides ideas for possible sections to include within the portfolio. It is suggested that a portfolio begin with an introductory section, which includes detailed information about the developer in terms of both background and beliefs.

1. **Introduction**
   - ❏ **Personal Statement.** Opening the portfolio with a personal, symbolic statement is recommended. A quote, poem, or brief statement that reflects beliefs related to education or children immediately sends a powerful message. This first piece can be an attention-getter, creatively presented, perhaps on a different, appealing, or colorful paper. Opening the portfolio with a symbolic statement adds a personal touch to the product.

   - ❏ **Resume.** Inclusion of a resume in the introductory section provides the viewer with a snapshot of a professional history, which includes reference to education and professional experience. A resume must be succinct and easy to read and scan so the viewer can gain an immediate impression about the creator and what qualifications she or he possesses. A one-page resume is generally desirable, but two pages are acceptable to best reflect all abilities.

     Particular attention to detail regarding the professional appearance of a resume is critical. A finished resume should be typed, free of spelling errors, and grammatically accurate. All information included in the resume must be factually accurate and honest in reflecting job-related qualifications. Make certain it is spell checked and proofread.

A basic resume should include the following:

- Job Objective
- Education/Training Acquired
- Work Experience or Work History
- Special Skills or Highlights or Related Volunteer Work
- Professional Affiliations and Membership in Professional Organizations
- References

When listing job or work experience, start with most recent position and work backward. Include dates and a *brief* statement regarding job duties. List three references available, but make sure to first obtain consent to use an individual as a reference. By contacting references ahead of time the likelihood of favorable recommendations is increased. Carefully proofread the finished document for accuracy. Sample resumes are provided in this manual. See pages 24–25.

❏ **Letters of Recommendation/Reference.** Letters of recommendation are necessary to verify skills and experience, using an authoritative outside source. Keep two points in mind when request-ing letters of reference. First, seek to obtain letters from those individuals who have been in a position to evaluate previous work. A letter from a school principal holds greater credibility than a letter from a fellow paraeducator. Second, letters of reference should be printed on official

school or agency letterhead. A letter of reference on letterhead confirms the authenticity of the document and renders it credible.

❏ **Acquired Skills Listing.** In a list format, enumerate and summarize specific skills acquired through either experience or training. A listing of special skills, beyond what might be included in the resume, makes it simple for the reviewer to quickly glean insight related to professional abilities and assess job-related qualifications and accomplishments. A list also helps the reviewer get to the point and can give focus to a discussion of job demands and matching personal qualifications. See the Acquired Skills Worksheet (p. 31) for further help in getting started with a listing. A sample Acquired Skills form (p. 30) is also provided to be of help in getting started.

❏ **Vision Statement.** Inclusion of a vision statement in an introductory section further develops and expresses one's personal role within the classroom as a caring, knowledgeable paraeducator. A vision statement should not be longer than one page in length and should describe the "vision" of the ideal classroom. Write about beliefs concerning student and teacher relationships, classroom climate, student-to-student learning, and student needs. Be sincere and to the point. Spend time developing and refining your vision statement over time. A format to begin might be: "My vision for the ideal classroom is . . . . I intend to help accomplish this by . . . ." Be prepared to address possible questions about your vision statement during a discussion related to your beliefs.

Sample Vision Statements

My vision for the ideal classroom is to help promote a positive educational opportunity where students will learn and grow.

- I will work with the teacher to challenge each student.
- I will enhance the environment by modeling respectful interactions.
- I will appreciate diversity and practice tolerance.

My vision is to assist all students to reach their potential:

- By having good relationships with other adults.
- By modeling good work habits.
- By improving my skills.
- By treating each child with dignity and respect.

My vision is to promote a positive educational opportunity for all students:

- By accepting each student.
- By having a good attitude.
- By working hard.
- By continually improving.

2. **Official Records**

   ❑ **Diploma.** Include photocopies of diplomas in the portfolio, rather than the original document.

   ❑ **Transcript.** Carefully consider whether or not to include a transcript in the portfolio especially if your grades do not best represent your abilities. If including a transcript, use a photocopy of an official document in the portfolio. Transcripts will be required upon obtaining a position.

❑ **Department of Public Instruction License.** If you have a state paraprofessional license, include a photocopy of the license in the portfolio.

❑ **Report Cards.** As with transcripts, give careful consideration to the inclusion of report cards in this section of the portfolio. Only exemplary grades should be included. A photocopy of grades earned from specific courses taken is verification of course completion and the quality of performance.

3. **Professional Development**

   ❑ **Formal Training.** The formal training section of the portfolio provides documentation of any higher education training received, workshop or seminar participation, conference attendance, or special certificates earned. Provide a summary list of continuing education training acquired and include photocopies of attendance certificates received. A reflective summary related to training should be included in the portfolio, describing what was learned and how the new knowledge in the classroom was applied. Documentation forms are included in the manual to either help relate new learning to standards or to guide the reflective process in general.

   ❑ **Professional Affiliations.** Belonging to professional organizations makes a statement about professionalism, interest, and dedication to the students. There are several organizations related to education and the special needs of learners, most of which provide informational newsletters and resources. If you belong to any particular organizations, create a statement indicating your affiliation with the organization and any specific involvement you might have had.

4. **Personal Philosophy Statements.** Personal philosophy statements provide a

snapshot of beliefs and values and express personal knowledge regarding best practices in education. For students in associate degree training programs, philosophy statements are generally required components of the training program. Condense personal philosophies into one-page statements, considering topic areas such as:

- Characteristics of an effective paraprofessional
- Classroom management philosophy
- Reading philosophy statement
- Education philosophy

For paraeducators working within the field, engage in a dialogue with other professionals with whom you work and seek insight regarding the philosophies adopted by your school district and how you have ascribed to those philosophies in your daily work with the students and parents you serve. Create a one-page summary describing your beliefs and review them with members of your teaching team. Include a final product in your portfolio.

5. **Work Samples/Artifacts.** A portfolio is enriched by the documents it incorporates as credible and concrete evidence of abilities. Both practicing paraeducators and the paraeducator students are in a position to consider including exemplary work samples that can speak a thousand words and "show off" how one has assisted students and teachers of the teaching team. Think about instructional strategies used on a regular basis and mastered, materials created or supports provided, and include actual artifacts or visuals of these products in the portfolio.

   ❑ **Photographs.** Include clearly focused photographs of games, materials, bulletin boards, or learning centers designed or created by you. Mount photos on paper used consistently throughout the portfolio and provide a brief, neatly typed, descriptive caption for each photograph. Summarize how the item was used and what skill the item was designed to enhance. Be certain to maintain confidentiality and anonymity of the work samples collected for the portfolio by not including names of students and other identifying information. Obtain permission before using photographs of students. A statement explaining that permission has been granted to use photographs would be appropriate and highly professional to display in the portfolio. A reviewer would recognize that the developer understands and practices confidentiality.

Sample Permission Form

_____ has my permission to use photographs of my child in her/his professional portfolio. I understand that no other identifying information will be distributed and that the photographs will not be used for profit.

Signed _____
Date _____

❑ **Videos.** Performance reviews or evaluations can be facilitated through the use of a videotape portraying a sample of an individual's instructional effectiveness. Specific skills or competencies can be viewed in-action through a video presentation. If a particular skill

Jane Smith
000 Main Street
Milwaukee, WI 53211
(000-222-3434)

Employment Objective

Seeking a paraprofessional position at the elementary school level.

Education

Community College Pewaukee, WI	Instructional Assistant Associate Degree Dean's List, National Honor Society	May 2003 Graduation

Experience

(Name) Elementary School Milwaukee, WI	Paraprofessional	August 2003–Present

Worked cooperatively with a teaching team serving students with multicategorical needs grades one through six. Supported students with significant learning needs and behavioral challenges within the inclusive setting, and worked with small instructional groups to reinforce academic skills. Facilitated communication between special education and general education teachers.

(Name) Elementary School Milwaukee, WI	Paraprofessional	June 2003–August 2003 Summer Program

Assisted within the districtwide summer school learning disabilities program. Provided daily small group instruction in reading and math using a direct instruction approach. Maintained a daily log of student performance and supervised recreational activities.

Volunteer Activities

Special Olympics Program, (Name) Street School Community First Program, Milwaukee, WI	Coach—After school activity Reading Tutor

References and Portfolio

Available upon request

Jane Smith
000 Main Street
Milwaukee, WI 53211
(000-222-3434)

Career Objective:	Position as a **Paraprofessional** in general education or special education, kindergarten through middle school.

Highlights of Qualification:

- Experienced in working with students with autism.
- Utilized augmentative/alternative communication.
- Effective in using positive classroom management techniques.
- Flexible in working within a diverse teaching team.
- Skilled in addressing sensory integrative needs of students.
- Knowledgeable of the IEP Process and goal integration.
- Developed computer expertise.

Related Experience:

(Name) Elementary School   **Paraprofessional**
Milwaukee, WI   August 2003–Present
Worked cooperatively with a teaching team serving students with severe communication needs, including autism. Facilitated the integration of IEP goals while working with individual students.

(Name) Elementary School   **Paraprofessional**
Milwaukee, WI   June 2003–August 2003
Assisted within the district-wide summer school learning disabilities program. Provided daily small group instruction in reading and math using a direct instruction approach. Maintained a daily log of student performance and supervised recreational activities.

Volunteer Activities:

Special Olympics Program, (Name) Street School   **Coach**
Community First Program, Milwaukee, WI   **Reading Tutor**

Employment History:

Company A, Milwaukee, WI   May 2000–June 2003
Accounts Payable Clerk

References and Portfolio

Available upon request

PORTFOLIO DEVELOPMENT CHECKLIST

Name: _____

1. Physical Properties

_____ Zip closure binder

_____ Divider pages with tabs

_____ Clear page protectors

2. Portfolio Introduction

_____ Introduction/reflection (personal statement, poem, quote . . .)

_____ Professional resume (heavy stock paper)

_____ Professional letters of recommendation (on school letterhead)

_____ Vision Statement

_____ Acquired Skills List

3. Official Records

_____ Diploma documentation (photocopy of diploma)

_____ Transcript

_____ Department of Public Instruction License (photocopy)

_____ Report cards (consider carefully)

4. Professional Development

_____ Formal training

❏ listing of completed college courses

❏ listing of degrees earned

❏ in-service training (reflection document, brochure)

❏ seminar, conference, or workshop participation (reflection document, brochure)

❏ related training: CPR, etc.

_____ Professional affiliations (professional organizations)

5. Personal Philosophy Statements (options to consider)

❏ characteristics of an effective paraprofessional

❏ classroom management philosophy

❏ reading philosophy statement

❏ education philosophy

❏ consider courses you've taken

❏ other

6. Work Samples/Artifacts (options to consider)

_____ Self-created games/materials (photos and written description)

_____ Self-created learning centers (photos and written description)

_____ Self-created bulletin boards (photos and written description)

_____ Artifacts from courses you have completed

_____ Videotape (video of you during instruction with critique)

_____ Forms created or used by you

❏ behavior monitoring forms

❏ academic recording forms

❏ study guides or outlines

❏ note-taking to support students

❏ *PowerPoint* presentations

❏ spreadsheets

❏ other

7. **Service Work**

_____ School related

❏ science fair

❏ folk fair

❏ career day

❏ school assemblies program

❏ family events (i.e., sock hop, talent show . . .)

_____ Community based (certificates, photos with captions, etc.)

❏ Special Olympics

❏ scouting

❏ coaching

❏ other

8. **Honors, Awards, Recognition** (photocopies, certificates, photos . . .)

_____ Scholastic

_____ School based

_____ Community based

9. **Professional Evaluations** (copies of actual documents)

_____ Performance evaluations from instructors

_____ Administrator evaluations

_____ Teacher feedback

_____ Self-evaluation

10. **Personals** (actual documents mounted on portfolio paper)

_____ Letters from parents

_____ Notes/letters from students

_____ Notes from coworkers

11. Goal Statements

_____ Goals related to academic training program

_____ Annual job-related goals

_____ Reflection related to the attainment of goals set

_____ Long-term goals (what might you do in five years?)

_____ Administrator input regarding goals

12. *No Child Left Behind*—Highly Qualified Documentation

_____ Reading _____
artifact

_____ Writing _____
artifact

_____ Math _____
artifact

13. Other: Topic/Document

_____ _____

_____ _____

_____ _____

_____ _____

_____ _____

_____ _____

_____ _____

Name _____ Date _____

My vision for the ideal classroom is to:

I will accomplish this by:

-

-

-

-

-

Signed _____

Permission Form—Photographs

_____ has my permission to use photographs of my child in her/his professional portfolio. I understand that no other identifying information will be distributed and that the photographs will not be used for profit.

Signed _____ Date _____

Permission Form—Photographs

_____ has my permission to use photographs of my child in her/his professional portfolio. I understand that no other identifying information will be distributed and that the photographs will not be used for profit.

Signed _____ Date _____

Permission Form—Photographs

_____ has my permission to use photographs of my child in her/his professional portfolio. I understand that no other identifying information will be distributed and that the photographs will not be used for profit.

Signed _____ Date _____

Permission Form—Photographs

_____ has my permission to use photographs of my child in her/his professional portfolio. I understand that no other identifying information will be distributed and that the photographs will not be used for profit.

Signed _____ Date _____

Permission Form—Work Samples

_____ has my permission to use work samples done by my child in her/his professional portfolio. I understand that no other identifying information will be distributed and that the work samples will not be used for profit.

Signed _____ Date _____

Permission Form—Work Samples

_____ has my permission to use work samples done by my child in her/his professional portfolio. I understand that no other identifying information will be distributed and that the work samples will not be used for profit.

Signed _____ Date _____

Permission Form—Work Samples

_____ has my permission to use work samples done by my child in her/his professional portfolio. I understand that no other identifying information will be distributed and that the work samples will not be used for profit.

Signed _____ Date _____

Permission Form—Work Samples

_____ has my permission to use work samples done by my child in her/his professional portfolio. I understand that no other identifying information will be distributed and that the work samples will not be used for profit.

Signed _____ Date _____

CHAPTER FIVE

Reflection

The Portfolio: A Tool in the Reflective Process

To reflect in a systematic way can be extremely helpful, satisfying, and is essential to professional development. Reflection requires looking at information, considering events that have happened, studying them, and then drawing conclusions to make changes in practice. Regular reflection facilitates a vision for future practice and allows one the opportunity to increase effectiveness. In order to reflect, one must set aside time in a calm place without interruptions. Clarity and presence of mind are necessary in enhancing the reflective process.

> Why not go out on a limb? Isn't that where the fruit is?
>
> —Frank Scully

Reflection should be the consistent practice of an educator and is imperative after an in-service or workshop training. The information must be recognized (What did I learn from this presentation?), integrated into the individual's previous learning or conceptions (How does this fit with what I already knew or have experienced?), evaluated (Is this something I value? Does it pertain to my situation?), and applied (How can I use this to enhance my performance?). Reflection is also necessary for on-the-job learning. When an incident happens the individual should consider what role he or she played, what was the effect, and what would he or she do differently? What is the desired result?

Students in training to become paraeducators are in a position to reflect on their learning, attitudes, readings from classes taken, and observations from practical experiences. As they construct their portfolios, they can use reflections and artifacts acquired during the course of their training. Reflective processing of new learning is often a required element of educational programs and expected of students in educational training programs.

For the portfolio, obviously, one must consider why an artifact or document is included. But it is the reflective process that makes the portfolio more than just a scrapbook. The paraeducator must ask, "What meaning does this artifact have? Why choose this item over something else? What do I have that documents I have met his goal or standard? What best illustrates that I have a specific skill or knowledge? What else do I need to learn? What does this artifact tell the viewer about me?

Included in the next section are forms to aid in reflection. The paraeducator may include them in the portfolio to give the reviewer context and insight into the paraeducator's thought process, as well as knowledge and skills.

The forms are based on professional development by targeting the competency the paraeducator is developing, what the paraeducator has done to develop that competency, and the paraeducator's practical application. Included are both sample and blank forms for the:

- *No Child Left Behind*'s highly qualified reading, writing, and mathematics requirements
- *Council for Exceptional Children Beginning Paraeducator Standards*
- Technology Assistants
- Library/Media Assistants

CEC Beginning Paraeducator Standard #9:
Professional and Ethical Practice

CEC

Knowledge:

PE9K2: Personal cultural biases and differences that affect one's ability to work with others.

What I did:

I attended a session at the state paraeducator conference on diversity.

What I learned:

I learned a lot! I learned that students from different cultures behave differently than I expect. Sometimes I think they are being disrespectful when actually they are being very polite. I learned that sometimes I am asking them to do things they don't understand and it is just a difference in culture.

How I will use what I learned
or
How I used what I learned:

I will be careful not to misinterpret student behavior. I will try to learn more about the students from different cultures in my class.

Signed: **Date:**

Documentation: Handouts or notes from session attended at conference.

CEC Beginning Paraeducator Standard #1:
Foundations

Knowledge:

PE1K1: Purposes of programs for individuals with exceptional learning needs.

What I did:

What I learned:

How I will use what I learned
or
How I used what I learned:

Signed: **Date:**

CEC Beginning Paraeducator Standard #1:
Foundations

Knowledge:

PE1K2: Basic educational terminology regarding students, programs, roles, and instructional activities.

What I did:

What I learned:

How I will use what I learned
or
How I used what I learned:

Signed: **Date:**

REFLECTION STATEMENT

CEC Beginning Paraeducator Standard #2:
Development and Characteristics of Learners

Knowledge:

PE2K1: Effects an exceptional condition(s) can have on an individual's life.

What I did:

What I learned:

How I will use what I learned
or
How I used what I learned:

Signed: **Date:**

CEC Beginning Paraeducator Standard #3:
Individual Learning Differences

Knowledge:

PE3K1: Rights and responsibilities of families and children as they relate to individual learning needs.

What I did:

What I learned:

How I will use what I learned
or
How I used what I learned:

Signed: **Date:**

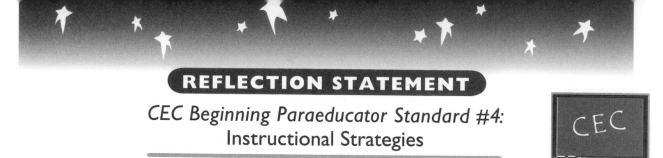

REFLECTION STATEMENT

CEC Beginning Paraeducator Standard #4:
Instructional Strategies

Knowledge:

PE4K1: Basic instructional and remedial strategies and materials.

What I did:

What I learned:

How I will use what I learned
or
How I used what I learned:

Signed: **Date:**

REFLECTION STATEMENT

CEC Beginning Paraeducator Standard #4:
Instructional Strategies

CEC

Knowledge:

PE4K2: Basic technologies appropriate to individuals with exceptional learning needs.

What I did:

What I learned:

How I will use what I learned
or
How I used what I learned:

Signed: **Date:**

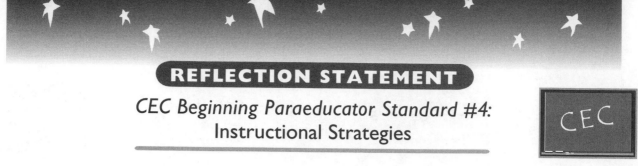

REFLECTION STATEMENT

CEC Beginning Paraeducator Standard #4:
Instructional Strategies

Skill:

PE4S1: Use strategies, equipment, materials, and techniques as directed to accomplish instructional objectives.

What I did:

What I learned:

How I will use what I learned
or
How I used what I learned:

Signed: **Date:**

REFLECTION STATEMENT

CEC Beginning Paraeducator Standard #4:
Instructional Strategies

Skill:

PE4S2: Assist in adapting instructional strategies and materials as directed.

What I did:

What I learned:

How I will use what I learned
or
How I used what I learned:

Signed: **Date:**

REFLECTION STATEMENT

CEC Beginning Paraeducator Standard #4:
Instructional Strategies

Skill:

PE4S3: Use strategies as directed to facilitate effective integration into various settings.

What I did:

What I learned:

How I will use what I learned
or
How I used what I learned:

Signed: **Date:**

CEC Beginning Paraeducator Standard #4:
Instructional Strategies

Skill:

PE4S4: Use strategies that promote the learner's independence as directed.

What I did:

What I learned:

How I will use what I learned
or
How I used what I learned:

Signed: **Date:**

CEC Beginning Paraeducator Standard #4:
Instructional Strategies

CEC

Skill:

PE4S5: Use strategies as directed to increase the individual's independence and confidence.

What I did:

What I learned:

How I will use what I learned
or
How I used what I learned:

Signed: **Date:**

CEC Beginning Paraeducator Standard #5:
Learning Environments and Social Interactions

Knowledge:

PE5K1: Demands of various learning environments.

What I did:

What I learned:

How I will use what I learned
or
How I used what I learned:

Signed: **Date:**

CEC Beginning Paraeducator Standard #5:
Learning Environments and Social Interactions

Knowledge:

PE5K2: Rules and procedural safeguards regarding the management of behaviors of individuals with exceptional learning needs.

What I did:

What I learned:

How I will use what I learned
or
How I used what I learned:

Signed: **Date:**

REFLECTION STATEMENT

CEC Beginning Paraeducator Standard #5:
Learning Environments and Social Interactions

CEC

Skill:

PE5S1: Establish and maintain rapport with learners.

What I did:

What I learned:

How I will use what I learned
or
How I used what I learned:

Signed: **Date:**

CEC Beginning Paraeducator Standard #5:
Learning Environments and Social Interactions

Skill:

PE5S2: Use universal precautions and assist in maintaining a safe, healthy learning environment.

What I did:

What I learned:

How I will use what I learned
or
How I used what I learned:

Signed: **Date:**

Skill:

PE5S3: Use strategies for managing behavior as directed.

What I did:

What I learned:

How I will use what I learned
or
How I used what I learned:

Signed: **Date:**

CEC Beginning Paraeducator Standard #5:
Learning Environments and Social Interactions

Skill:

PE5S4: Use strategies as directed, in a variety of settings, to assist in the development of social skills.

What I did:

What I learned:

How I will use what I learned
or
How I used what I learned:

Signed: **Date:**

Knowledge:

PE6K1: Characteristics of appropriate communication with stakeholders.

What I did:

What I learned:

How I will use what I learned
or
How I used what I learned:

Signed: **Date:**

REFLECTION STATEMENT

CEC Beginning Paraeducator Standard #7:
Instructional Planning

Knowledge:

PE7K1: Follow written plans, seeking clarification as needed.

What I did:

What I learned:

How I will use what I learned
or
How I used what I learned:

Signed: **Date:**

CEC Beginning Paraeducator Standard #7:
Instructional Planning

Skill:

PE7S1: Prepare and organize materials to support teaching and learning as directed.

What I did:

What I learned:

How I will use what I learned
or
How I used what I learned:

Signed: **Date:**

REFLECTION STATEMENT

CEC Beginning Paraeducator Standard #8: Assessment

Knowledge:

PE8K1: Rationale for assessment.

What I did:

What I learned:

How I will use what I learned
or
How I used what I learned:

Signed: **Date:**

CEC Beginning Paraeducator Standard #8:
Assessment

Skill:

PE8S1: Demonstrate basic collection techniques as directed.

What I did:

What I learned:

How I will use what I learned
or
How I used what I learned:

Signed: **Date:**

Skill:

PE8S2: Make and document objective observations.

What I did:

What I learned:

How I will use what I learned
or
How I used what I learned:

Signed: **Date:**

CEC Beginning Paraeducator Standard #9:
Professional and Ethical Practice

Knowledge:

PE9K1: Ethical practices for confidential communication about individuals with exceptional learning needs.

What I did:

What I learned:

How I will use what I learned
or
How I used what I learned:

Signed: **Date:**

Knowledge:

PE9K2: Personal cultural biases and differences that affect one's ability to work with others.

What I did:

What I learned:

How I will use what I learned
or
How I used what I learned:

Signed: **Date:**

CEC Beginning Paraeducator Standard #9:
Professional and Ethical Practice

Skill:

PE9S1: Perform responsibilities as directed in a manner consistent with laws and policies.

What I did:

What I learned:

How I will use what I learned
or
How I used what I learned:

Signed: **Date:**

Skill:

PE9S2: Follow instructions of the professional.

What I did:

What I learned:

How I will use what I learned
or
How I used what I learned:

Signed: **Date:**

Skill:

PE9S3: Demonstrate problem-solving, flexible thinking, conflict management techniques, and analysis of personal strengths and preferences.

What I did:

What I learned:

How I will use what I learned
or
How I used what I learned:

Signed: **Date:**

Skill:

PE9S4: Act as a role model for individuals with exceptional learning needs.

What I did:

What I learned:

How I will use what I learned
or
How I used what I learned:

Signed: **Date:**

CEC Beginning Paraeducator Standard #9: Professional and Ethical Practice

Skill:

PE9S5: Demonstrate commitment to assisting learners in achieving their highest potential.

What I did:

What I learned:

How I will use what I learned
or
How I used what I learned:

Signed: **Date:**

CEC Beginning Paraeducator Standard #9:
Professional and Ethical Practice

CEC

Skill:

PE9S6: Demonstrate the ability to separate personal issues from one's responsibilities as a paraeducator.

What I did:

What I learned:

How I will use what I learned
or
How I used what I learned:

Signed: **Date:**

Skill:

PE9S7: Maintain a high level of competence and integrity.

What I did:

What I learned:

How I will use what I learned
or
How I used what I learned:

Signed: **Date:**

REFLECTION STATEMENT

CEC Beginning Paraeducator Standard #9:
Professional and Ethical Practice

Skill:

PE9S8: Exercise objective and prudent judgment.

What I did:

What I learned:

How I will use what I learned
or
How I used what I learned:

Signed: **Date:**

Skill:

PE9S9: Demonstrate proficiency in academic skills, including oral and written communication.

What I did:

What I learned:

How I will use what I learned
or
How I used what I learned:

Signed: **Date:**

REFLECTION STATEMENT

CEC Beginning Paraeducator Standard #9:
Professional and Ethical Practice

Skill:

PE9S10: Engage in activities to increase one's own knowledge and skills.

What I did:

What I learned:

How I will use what I learned
or
How I used what I learned:

Signed: **Date:**

Skill:

PE9S11: Engage in self-assessment.

What I did:

What I learned:

How I will use what I learned
or
How I used what I learned:

Signed: **Date:**

REFLECTION STATEMENT

CEC Beginning Paraeducator Standard #9:
Professional and Ethical Practice

CEC

Skill:

PE9S12: Accept and use constructive feedback.

What I did:

What I learned:

How I will use what I learned
or
How I used what I learned:

Signed: **Date:**

REFLECTION STATEMENT

CEC Beginning Paraeducator Standard #10:
Collaboration

Knowledge:

PE10K1: Common concerns of families of individuals with exceptional learning needs.

What I did:

What I learned:

How I will use what I learned
or
How I used what I learned:

Signed: **Date:**

REFLECTION STATEMENT

CEC Beginning Paraeducator Standard #10:
Collaboration

CEC

Knowledge:

PE10K2: Roles of stakeholders in planning an individualized program.

What I did:

What I learned:

How I will use what I learned
or
How I used what I learned:

Signed: **Date:**

CEC Beginning Paraeducator Standard #10:
Collaboration

Skill:

PE10S1: Assist in collecting and providing objective, accurate information to professionals.

What I did:

What I learned:

How I will use what I learned
or
How I used what I learned:

Signed: **Date:**

CEC Beginning Paraeducator Standard #10:
Collaboration

CEC

Skill:

PE10S2: Collaborate with stakeholders as directed.

What I did:

What I learned:

How I will use what I learned
or
How I used what I learned:

Signed: **Date:**

CEC Beginning Paraeducator Standard #10:
Collaboration

Skill:

PE10S3: Foster respectful and beneficial relationships.

What I did:

What I learned:

How I will use what I learned
or
How I used what I learned:

Signed: **Date:**

CEC Beginning Paraeducator Standard #10:
Collaboration

Skill:

PE10S4: Participate as directed in conferences as a member of the educational team.

What I did:

What I learned:

How I will use what I learned
or
How I used what I learned:

Signed: **Date:**

CEC Beginning Paraeducator Standard #10: Collaboration

CEC

Skill:

PE10S5: Function in a manner that demonstrates a positive regard for the distinctions between roles and responsibilities of paraeducators and those of professionals.

What I did:

What I learned:

How I will use what I learned
or
How I used what I learned:

Signed: **Date:**

REFLECTION STATEMENT
Technology Assistant

Indicator I:

Demonstrate a sound understanding of technology operations and concepts.

What I did:

What I learned:

How I will use what I learned
or
How I used what I learned:

Signed: **Date:**

REFLECTION STATEMENT
Technology Assistant

Indicator II:

Assist teachers in planning and designing effective learning environments and experiences supported by technology.

What I did:

What I learned:

How I will use what I learned
or
How I used what I learned:

Signed: **Date:**

Indicator III:

Assist teachers in implementing curriculum plans that include methods and strategies for applying technology to maximize student learning.

What I did:

What I learned:

How I will use what I learned
or
How I used what I learned:

Signed: **Date:**

REFLECTION STATEMENT
Technology Assistant

Indicator IV:

Assist teachers in applying technology to facilitate a variety of effective assessment and evaluation strategies.

What I did:

What I learned:

How I will use what I learned
or
How I used what I learned:

Signed: **Date:**

REFLECTION STATEMENT
Technology Assistant

Indicator V:

Assist teachers in using technology to enhance their productivity and professional practices.

What I did:

What I learned:

How I will use what I learned
or
How I used what I learned:

Signed: **Date:**

Technology Assistant

Indicator VI:

Understand the social, ethical, legal, and human issues surrounding the use of technology in PK–12 schools and apply that understanding to practice.

What I did:

What I learned:

How I will use what I learned
or
How I used what I learned:

Signed: **Date:**

REFLECTION STATEMENT
Library/Media Center Assistant V

Indicator:

Develop knowledge and skills related to duties.

What I did:

What I learned:

How I will use what I learned
or
How I used what I learned:

Signed: **Date:**

CHAPTER SIX

Evaluating the Portfolio: Phase IV

Putting It to the Test

Before entering into an actual interview or review situation, first share the portfolio with others. Perhaps select a trusted peer or member of the teaching team. Ask for honest, constructive feedback related to overall impressions of the portfolio and suggestions for improvement. Simulate the interview or review session and practice displaying the portfolio while discussing contents. A mock interview or review session with an administrator would be ideal.

Thoughtfully consider feedback obtained and make any adjustments or additions necessary to enhance the quality or functionality of the portfolio. A Feedback Form (p. 100) is included in the manual for this purpose. Copy the form and distribute it to individuals willing

> Opportunities are often things you haven't noticed the first time around.
> —Catherine Deneuve

to view and critique the work. Be open, yet not tied, to suggestions. Remember the portfolio will be unique and the developer has the final say about what is included.

On an annual basis, repeat the phases (1) brainstorming; (2) gathering the evidence; (3) organizing. Reflect upon the year you have had, what you have learned, and how you have grown. Record new training, new experiences, and document new insights through a reflective piece. Discuss how to apply new knowledge in the educational setting. Engage in self-evaluation to determine what stays in the portfolio, what will be added, and what will be used to replace previous work samples. Only those samples that are considered best should remain. Consider the portfolio a dynamic tool, subject to change as the creator grows as a professional.

PORTFOLIO FEEDBACK FORM

Name: _____ Date Viewed: _____

Overall Impression: _____
_____
_____
_____
_____

Strengths Noted: _____
_____
_____
_____
_____
_____

Suggestions for Improvement: _____
_____
_____
_____
_____
_____

Comments: _____
_____
_____
_____
_____
_____

Thanks so much for your feedback! _____

CHAPTER SEVEN

How Does One Use the Portfolio?

Using Your Portfolio

Using a portfolio during an interview, performance evaluation, or upon completion of coursework can help concretely display talents, interests, achievements, and experiences, thus making the developer's inherent worth more apparent and clear to the reviewer. Further, the portfolio can open the door to discussion based on abilities and experiences and can offer structure to the review process. Many paraeducators have commented on how their portfolios have saved them when they were at a loss for words during an interview or review. In a sense, the portfolio can speak for the creator and is worth a thousand words.

The question often arises, "How do I use my portfolio during a job interview or performance evaluation?" Of course, there is no single answer to this question. Each situation is unique and calls for different action. Recognizing the dynamic nature of an interview or an evaluation, it is best to flow with the process and present the portfolio or sections of the portfolio at opportune times during the discussion. For example, when asked about beliefs regarding education, turn to the philosophy or vision statements and provide a summary of beliefs. The document should not be read to the reviewer, but should serve as a guide and a reference point during the course of a conversation. It helps to cover the key points, outlined and organized by the developer. The document helps the interviewee or individual being evaluated recall desired information, maintain composure and confidently relate critical information in a clear fashion.

> We work not only to produce but to give value to time.
>
> —Eugene Delacroix

Portfolios can also be used when inevitable requests present themselves: "So, tell me about yourself" or "What have you accomplished this year?" It may be advantageous to take a systematic approach and proceed through the portfolio section by section and point out highlights. Or another strategy is to skim or skip sections of the portfolio and concentrate on more relevant or stronger sections that specifically relate to inquisitions of the reviewer. By having a well-organized portfolio and knowing it well, the portfolio becomes a powerful tool to present the developer in the most advantageous manner possible.

Advance preparation for an interview or an evaluation will also assist in confidently approaching the session. Enter a portfolio discussion knowing the goals and needs of the school or organization. Study the school's vision or mission statements. The applicant should seek out this critical information and consider how her or his skills align with the basic philosophical constructs of the educational organization. Select and present portfolio documents that best illustrate how the interviewee's knowledge and skills are consistent with the employer needs or ideals. If the portfolio is used as a performance review for a student in training, be clear on course objectives and requirements for demonstrated competence. As a working paraeducator, know the job description and expectations, professional development goals, and the needs of students and the teaching team. Show concrete work samples or documents and explain projects completed and implemented with success as they relate to professional goals and course work. Share letters of reference or thank you notes that speak to interpersonal skills and team-oriented job focus. Remember, the portfolio is a way of marketing or representing an individual. It is a powerful tool that speaks *for* the paraeducator *about* the paraeducator.

To further prepare for an interview using the portfolio, it can be advantageous to arrange for a practice or mock interview. It is generally best to attempt to simulate, as much as possible, a typical interview experience by meeting with someone who is in a supervisory position or who is capable of evaluating the paraeducator's work. Students in training programs are encouraged to seek an interview with a program instructor or with a school administrator or supervising teacher at a field placement site. Working paraeducators may practice interviewing with a supervising teacher, team leader, or administrative representative. A list of typical interview questions is provided in this manual. Read through the questions and plan likely responses. Reflect on how to integrate the use of the portfolio and practice doing so.

Interview and Evaluation Strategy

When preparing for an interview or a job performance evaluation, think of three or four success stories like the ones below. These must be actual, true events that reflect your abilities and commitment.

One day I was working with a student who was having difficulty remembering the spelling of a science word. I made up a sentence so that the first letter in each word, in order, was a letter in the science word. He still remembers how to spell the word and the other day he told me he now makes up sentences to spell difficult words. He learned that from me.

Three girls in our classroom like American Girl dolls. My daughter subscribes to the

American Girl magazine and I bring her old copies to school for the girls to read. They were not interested in reading until I started bringing in the magazines. Now they read them over and over.

Two boys were screaming at each other in the hallway. One accused the other of bothering his girlfriend. The other one denied it but was calling her names. I thought they were going to punch each other any second. Then I remembered my CPI training and I was able to de-escalate the situation. Eventually I got them to shake hands and walk away.

SAMPLE
Paraeducator Interview Questions

1. Why do you want to work as a paraeducator? Why are you interested in this position?

2. What do you see as the role of the paraeducator working as a team member with a teacher or group of teachers?

3. What qualities do you possess that make you a good candidate for this job?

4. What are some classroom management strategies you'd use to *prevent* misbehavior in the classroom?

5. What are some classroom management strategies you'd use in *responding* to misbehavior in the classroom?

6. What would you do when the lesson is completed and you have extra time?

7. Describe your working style. Do you prefer a daily routine? Do you prefer working from a list? Through verbal instructions?

8. If you disagreed with something going on in the classroom, how would you try to change it?

9. Suppose there is a severe home problem that is affecting the child at school. A neighbor comes to you and wants to know what's going on. How do you respond? Why?

10. Suppose a parent approaches you and wants to know specific details regarding the teacher's teaching and classroom management style. How would you respond?

11. What are your strengths? What are your weaknesses?

12. Tell us about some reading strategies you might use to help a child with a reading disability.

13. What experiences have you had that might enhance your ability to support special education needs students in the general education classroom?

14. How might you build student self-esteem?

15. What would you do if you observed a student bullying another student?

16. What is your philosophy of education?

CHAPTER EIGHT

How Does One Plan Professional Development?

Goal Setting: Professional Development Plans

Goal setting is a critical component to successful professional development, job satisfaction, and effective performance, whether you are a practicing paraeducator or a student in a training program. "If you don't know where you are going, you might end up somewhere else." Goal-oriented planning sets the stage for a journey of continuous improvement and fulfillment. It encourages focused, proactive planning by establishing priorities and monitoring growth. Inclusion of professional goals in the portfolio process demonstrates professional dedication and a commitment to self-improvement.

> Enthusiasm is mental sunshine that keeps everything in us alive and growing.
>
> —Unknown

Establishing goals can be done in several ways. They can be based on:

- **Performance evaluations.** Goals may be determined through an annual evaluation process and based on areas designated as needing improvement. For example, during an evaluation, feedback is given to improve behavior management skills. Part of the next professional development plan should include attention to improving behavior management skills. You can use the portfolio process to document that you have taken the needed training and reflected on what you learned, how you will use it, and provided evidence of your increased skills as a part of an improvement plan.

- **Student needs, especially those outlined in Individual Education Programs.** The reason you have been hired is to help meet the needs of students. To center your professional development plan on the needs of the students you serve is necessary to their success and yours. For example, if you have a student whose IEP included using American Sign Language to communicate, learning how to communicate with the student using American Sign Language or perhaps building a sign language repertoire would be an appropriate and necessary goal for you.

- **Job descriptions.** Often job descriptions for paraeducators are fairly generic, referring mainly to "other duties as assigned," but most do refer to following district and building policies. In that case a goal might be to learn the district and building policies. You might use the portfolio process to document that you know the policies by including a reflective statement and a copy of the policy manual in which you have highlighted the parts most pertinent to your job. If you have a more specific job description that accurately describes what you do, you can use it to help establish your goals. For example, for a job description that states you will be doing tube feedings, setting a goal of learning this procedure would be a high priority. For a job description with an expectation for effective communication, create a goal to establish a pattern of communication that is consistent and accurate.

- **Standards or competencies.** Several states have standards for paraeducators and many are in the process of setting standards.

- The Council for Exceptional Children (CEC) has a set of performance-based standards for beginning paraeducators. Paraeducators may want to use these standards for a basis. Once the paraeducator has gained experience, goal setting may be based more specifically on job requirements and feedback from supervisors and coworkers. (See form on page 116.) The CEC standards are divided into ten knowledge and skills areas:

    1. Foundations
    2. Development and characteristics of learners
    3. Individual learning differences
    4. Instructional strategies
    5. Learning environments/Social interactions
    6. Language
    7. Instructional planning
    8. Assessment
    9. Professional and ethical practice
    10. Collaboration

    The CEC standards can be found at www.cec.sped.org and at the end of this section.

- The National Resource Center for Paraprofessionals has published a set of competencies that address knowledge and skills and are divided into levels for proficiency titled *Strengthening and Supporting Teacher/Provider Paraeducator Teams: Guidelines for Paraeducator Roles, Supervision, and Preparation* by Anna Lou Pickett. To obtain a copy access the resource center website at www.nrcpara.org.

- The National Education Association in their *Paraeducator Handbook* identifies basic competencies, skills, and knowledge including: roles and responsibilities, communications, behavior management, growth and development/ psychology, legal and ethical issues, instructional strategies, and diversity and equity. The handbook also lists competencies for paraeducators working in specialized programs such as early childhood, technology, and English as a second language. The handbook can be downloaded at www.nea.org.

- The American Federation of Teachers (AFT) offers two publications on standards, *Standards for a Profession* and *Skill Standards for Education Paraprofessionals*. See the AFT website for further information, www.aft.org.

- **A combination of any of the above**

- **Students in paraeducator training programs.** For students in paraeducator training programs, goal setting is often a required component of the curriculum

and may revolve around specific program competencies or identified areas of need. Other goals could be designed to meet the demands within a field placement, where child and program specific issues are present. For students in training, instructors and cooperating teachers should assist in targeting meaningful goals. A comprehensive self-assessment, combined with feedback, can reveal strengths and weaknesses and drive the goal-setting process. Through reflection the student in training creates goals that will enhance growth and professional development.

An Individual Improvement Plan form is provided in this manual to assist in starting the goal-setting process. See the sample Paraeducator Professional Development Goals sheet (following) for an example to formally state and display goals within the portfolio.

CEC Knowledge and Skill Base
for All Beginning Special Education Paraeducators

Special Education Standard #1: Foundations

Knowledge:	
PE1K1	Purposes of programs for individuals with exceptional learning needs.
PE1K2	Basic educational terminology regarding students, programs, roles, and instructional activities.
Skills:	

Special Education Standard #2: Development and Characteristics of Learners

Knowledge:	
PE2K1	Effects an exceptional condition(s) can have on an individual's life.
Skills:	

Special Education Standard #3: Individual Learning Differences

Knowledge:	
PE3K1	Rights and responsibilities of families and children as they relate to individual learning needs.
PE3K2	Indicators of abuse and neglect.
Skills:	
PE3S1	Demonstrate sensitivity to the diversity of individuals and families.

Special Education Standard #4: Instructional Strategies

Knowledge:	
PE4K1	Basic instructional and remedial strategies and materials.
PE4K2	Basic technologies appropriate to individuals with exceptional learning needs.
Skills:	
PE4S1	Use strategies, equipment, materials, and technologies, as directed, to accomplish instructional objectives.
PE4S2	Assist in adapting instructional strategies and materials as directed.
PE4S3	Use strategies as directed to facilitate effective integration into various settings.

PE4S4	Use strategies that promote the learner's independence as directed.
PE4S5	Use strategies as directed to increase the individual's independence and confidence.

Special Education Standard #5: Learning Environments and Social Interactions

Knowledge:	
PE5K1	Demands of various learning environments.
PE5K2	Rules and procedural safeguards regarding the management of behaviors of individuals with exceptional learning needs.

Skills:	
PE5S1	Establish and maintain rapport with learners.
PE5S2	Use universal precautions and assist in maintaining a safe, healthy learning environment.
PE5S3	Use stragegies for managing behavior as directed.
PE5S4	Use strategies as directed, in a variety of settings, to assist in the development of social skills.

Special Education Standard #6: Language

Knowledge:	
PE6K1	Characteristics of appropriate communication with stakeholders.
Skills:	

Special Education Standard #7: Instructional Planning

Knowledge:	
Skills:	
PE7S1	Follow written plans, seeking clarification as needed.
PE7S2	Prepare and organize materials to support teaching and learning as directed.

Special Education Standard #8: Assessment

Knowledge:	
PE8K1	Rationale for assessment.
Skills:	
PE8S1	Demonstrate basic collection techniques as directed.
PE8S2	Make and document objective observations as directed.

Continues on next page

Special Education Standard #9: Professional and Ethical Practice

Knowledge:	
PE9K1	Ethical practices for confidential communication about individuals with exceptional learning needs.
PE9K2	Personal cultural biases and differences that affect one's ability to work with others.
Skills:	
PE9S1	Perform responsibilities as directed in a manner consistent with laws and policies.
PE9S2	Follow instructions of the professional.
PE9S3	Demonstrate problem-solving, flexible thinking, conflict management techniques, and analysis of personal strengths and preferences.
PE9S4	Act as a role model for individuals with exceptional learning needs.
PE9S5	Demonstrate commitment to assisting learners in achieving their highest potential.
PE9S6	Demonstrate the ability to separate personal issues from one's responsibilities as a paraeducator.
PE9S7	Maintain a high level of competence and integrity.
PE9S8	Exercise objective and prudent judgment.
PE9S9	Demonstrate proficiency in academic skills, including oral and written communication.
PE9S10	Engage in activities to increase one's own knowledge and skills.
PE9S11	Engage in self-assessment.
PE9S12	Accept and use constructive feedback.
PE9S13	Demonstrate ethical practices as guided by the CEC Code of Ethics and other standards and policies.

Special Education Standard #10: Collaboration

Knowledge:	
PE10K1	Common concerns of families of individuals with exceptional learning needs.
PE10K2	Roles of stakeholders in planning an individualized program.
Skills:	
PE10S1	Assist in collecting and providing objective, accurate information to professionals.
PE10S2	Collaborate with stakeholders as directed.

PE10S3	Foster respectful and beneficial relationships.
PE10S4	Participate as directed in conferences as members of the education team.
PE10S5	Function in a manner that demonstrates a positive regard for the distinctions between roles and responsibilities of paraeducators and those of professionals.

Paraeducator Professional Development Goals

Goal: *To increase my knowledge of sign language*

Goal: *To learn appropriate behavioral techniques*

Goal: *To become skilled working on the computer*

Goal: *To practice effective communication techniques*

Goal: *To maintain a positive attitude when working with students with disruptive behaviors*

Individual Improvement Plan

Name _____ Date _____

List three of your knowledge/skill area strengths:

1. *I relate well to students. Students like me.*

2. *I have good work habits. I am on time, dress appropriately, etc.*

3. *I am very organized.*

List three knowledge/skill areas you would like to improve	Steps to Take	Completion Date	Portfolio Documentation
1. To increase my knowledge of sign language	*1. Take a community education class on sign language*	*January 15*	*Certificate of attendance from class. Reflective statement on what was learned and its application.*
2. To learn appropriate behavioral techniques.	*1. Study handout provided by education district EBD specialist.*	*November 1*	*Reflective statement on what was learned and how to use it. Observation statement from teacher.*
3. To become skilled on the computer.	*1. Work with technology assistant to learn PowerPoint.*	*February 20*	*PowerPoint printout and reflective statement.*

Individual Improvement Plan

Name _____ Date _____

List three of your knowledge/skill area strengths:

1.

2.

3.

List three knowledge/ skill areas you would like to improve	Steps to Take	Completion Date	Portfolio Documentation

SAMPLE PROFESSIONAL DEVELOPMENT PLAN

Based on Council for Exceptional Children Standards for Beginning Paraeducators

CEC

Name _____

Standard 1: Foundations	Training Activity	Portfolio Documentation	Projected Completion Date
Know the purposes of programs for individuals with exceptional learning needs.	Meeting with Special Education Director	Reflective summary	October 1

Standard 2: Development and characteristics of learners	Training Activity	Portfolio Documentation	Projected Completion Date
Know the effects an exceptional condition(s) can have on an individual's life.	Meeting with Special Education Director	Reflective summary	October 1

Standard 3: Individual learning differences	Training Activity	Portfolio Documentation	Projected Completion Date
Know indicators of abuse and neglect.	Attend in-service training on indicators of abuse and neglect given by school social worker and school nurse.	Handouts from in-service	January 1

Standard 4: Instructional strategies	Training Activity	Portfolio Documentation	Projected Completion Date
Assist in adapting instructional strategies and materials as directed.	Read handbook on implementing adaptations	Log of adaptations made as directed by teacher	January 1

Name _____

Standard 1: Foundations	Training Activity	Portfolio Documentation	Projected Completion Date

Standard 2: Development and characteristics of learners	Training Activity	Portfolio Documentation	Projected Completion Date

Standard 3: Individual learning differences	Training Activity	Portfolio Documentation	Projected Completion Date

Standard 4: Instructional strategies	Training Activity	Portfolio Documentation	Projected Completion Date

Standard 5: Learning environments/ social interactions	Training Activity	Portfolio Documentation	Projected Completion Date

Standard 6: Language	Training Activity	Portfolio Documentation	Projected Completion Date

Standard 7: Instructional planning	Training Activity	Portfolio Documentation	Projected Completion Date

Standard 8: Assessment	Training Activity	Portfolio Documentation	Projected Completion Date

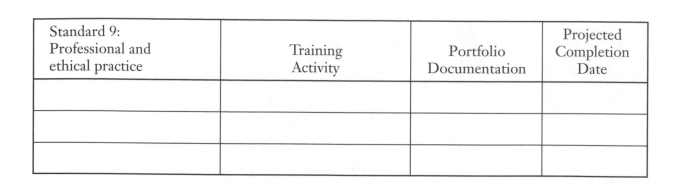

Standard 9: Professional and ethical practice	Training Activity	Portfolio Documentation	Projected Completion Date

Standard 10: Collaboration	Training Activity	Portfolio Documentation	Projected Completion Date

PROFESSIONAL DEVELOPMENT PLAN

Based on *No Child Left Behind* Requirements

NCLB

Name _____ Date _____

Goal I
To improve my ability to assist in teaching reading I will:

Date completed _____

Goal 2
To improve my ability to assist in teaching writing I will:

Date completed _____

Goal 3
To improve my ability to assist in teaching mathematics I will:

Date completed _____

Goal 4
To improve my ability to _____ I will:

Date completed _____

Signature _____

Professional Development— Organizing a Team

A support team is ideal to help with goal setting, providing training, and giving feedback. Membership on the team can include anyone who works with the paraeducator to achieve the desired outcomes for the students. An essential member is the building or program administrator who gets the team started. Other professionals and staff may participate depending on the requirements of the paraeducator's job, but the core of the team is the classroom teacher and the paraeducator.

Support Team Membership

Member	Roles	Responsibilities
Administrator	• Initiator • Supporter • Evaluator	• Starts the team • Supports members • Evaluates progress
Special Education Teacher	• Team and classroom leader • Trainer • Facilitator • Evaluator	• Leads the team • Organizes the meetings • Identifies areas of need • Provides training to the paraeducator • Facilitates other training opportunities • Verifies standards met
Paraeducator	• Learner • Documenter • Self-evaluator	• Receives training • Identifies areas for development • Self-evaluates performance • Demonstrates competence • Develops portfolio
Others working with the paraeducator, e.g., regular education teacher, school nurse, experienced paraeducator, physical therapist.	• Trainer • Supporter • Evaluator	• Identifies areas of need • Provides training • Facilitates training • Verifies standards met

From *Paraeducator Support Teams: Blueprint for Success* (2001) by Carol A. Long and Mark Dyar, published by Cooperative Educational Service Agency #4, West Salem, Wisconsin.

How Does One Create an Electronic Portfolio?

Presenting Electronic Portfolios

Some districts, states, and institutions of higher education are requiring electronic portfolios. Instead of keeping materials in a binder, a computer is used to preserve a digitized version of the portfolio. The electronic portfolio has the same components as a binder portfolio, but the contents may be stored on a computer drive, a diskette, or, perhaps, a compact disk (CD).

> Every day, in every way, I'm getting better and better.
>
> —Emile Coulé

Presenting a portfolio in an electronic format can be a practical, effective way to showcase knowledge and skills. First, electronic portfolios are compact. An entire portfolio can be saved to a hard drive, disk, or CD, and multiple copies can be kept at different locations for safekeeping. Electronic portfolios are easy to transport. Many formats can be emailed and, therefore, are very convenient for prospective employers. An electronic portfolio can also be posted to a website and viewed by numerous people who have access to the site. And it can always be printed out for a hard copy version. Second, an electronic portfolio makes a very positive statement about one's technology skills by telling the reviewer that the creator is up to date with technology and able to translate those skills into practical applications. Finally, it gives the portfolio a professional appearance and can be projected for formal presentations with an LCD projector.

Creating Electronic Portfolios

Creating an electronic portfolio involves basically the same process as developing a binder portfolio. However, an additional layer of complexity is included that requires taking the same material and putting it in an electronic format. Electronic portfolios can range from relatively simple, using *PowerPoint*, to highly complex, using programs such as *Authorware*.

Steps to follow:

1. If it is required that you create an electronic portfolio, before beginning check with the district, state, or institution of higher education to learn the software and format requirements. Using the correct software and format from the start will save many headaches down the road. Some districts or states may even have templates to use that will save time and frustration.

2. Find out what equipment is available and when it is available. For example, can the school computer lab be used before or after school? Is the equipment compatible? Will the scanner work with the computer? Here is an example of an important question: "I want to use my personal computer at home for word processing but store my work on the computer at school. I'll use a disk or email to transfer the files. Is my word processing program at home compatible with the word processing program on the computers at work?" Another  question might be: "The school digital camera requires a floppy disk but my computer only has a CD drive. What do I do?"

3. Find out who is available for assistance and when. Can the school computer technician help? Is there someone who has created an electronic portfolio and is willing to answer questions?

4. Learn the necessary skills. Consider the following:
   - Word processing
   - Scanning
   - Digital photography
   - Digital video
   - Voice synthesizing
   - Requirements of specific software such as creating slides, background design, and transitioning for *PowerPoint*; linking pages for *FrontPage*; or resizing, cropping, and erasing for *Photoshop*.
   - Importing images and graphics

   Step 4 can be part of the paraeducator's professional development plan to increase technology skills. Development of an electronic portfolio may require and result in the development of new technology skills. These skills can be documented as evidence of continuing professional development in the area of technology. The form on page 125 is designed to plan and document technology skills and can be used as an artifact in the portfolio.

5. Develop a binder version of the portfolio first and then transfer it to electronic format. This is suggested for two reasons. First, a binder version will be needed to store the original documents and may still be used during face-to-face interviews. Second, the binder version will also serve as a template for the electronic version and acquaint the developer with the portfolio process without the complexities of trying to manipulate the technology. Having a concrete portfolio provides the developer with a visual of the product or the "big picture" to help in sorting through information while developing the electronic counterpart.

6. Consider how to structure the electronic portfolio. An advantage of creating an

PowerPoint storyboard

Interactive storyboard

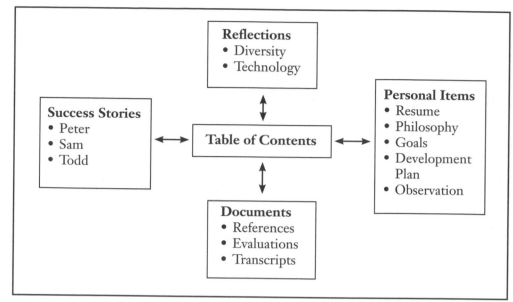

Reflections
• Diversity
• Technology

Success Stories
• Peter
• Sam
• Todd

Table of Contents

Personal Items
• Resume
• Philosophy
• Goals
• Development Plan
• Observation

Documents
• References
• Evaluations
• Transcripts

electronic version is that the portfolio can be interactive. This is another way of saying the pages can be linked, in the same way as a set of web pages. The reviewer does not have to progress through the portfolio in a linear fashion but can click from one section to another, skipping sections if wanted. For example, depending on the software used, each professional development goal can be linked directly to the reflection statement and documentation that corresponds to that goal. The table of contents can be formatted so each item is directly linked to the corresponding section.

This takes a great deal of planning and organization. Using a storyboard can be an effective method for structuring the electronic portfolio. The storyboard allows the developer to map out or plan the structure of the portfolio screen by screen, and allow the developer to view and manipulate different pages as desired.

7. When converting to an electronic format, start simple and add special features later such as transitioning, sound effects, music, or animation. But KEEP IT SIMPLE. Do not distract the reviewer with needless clutter or interruptions.

8. Keep in mind that like all portfolios, the electronic portfolio process is ongoing and the portfolio must be updated. Update with content and with newly learned technology skills. For example, if the para-educator has learned how to collect data and graph it using an electronic spreadsheet, a sample spreadsheet could be scanned in or imported into the electronic portfolio, thus demonstrating several new skills.

Creativity can flourish in the electronic portfolio through graphics, photographs, and individual materials. Graphics, as simple as an icon or picture of a pencil in the corner of each page, can add continuity and detail that enhance the portfolio and make it a pleasurable experience to review. Photographs, as in a traditional binder, give the portfolio realism and personalize the experience. Digital photographs are easy to manipulate so they fit the available space and convey the desired affect. Though the electronic portfolio adds another layer of complexity to the portfolio process, it can present the contents in a highly professional, polished manner that accurately reflects the creator's knowledge and skills.

TECHNOLOGY SKILLS DEVELOPMENT WORKSHEET

Skill	Current level: Novice, Adequate, Proficient	Resource(s) for development	Target date for proficiency	Date when desired competency is reached
Word processing				
Scanner				
Digital camera				
Image manipulating				
Voice synthesizing				
Multimedia presentations				
Web page development				
Importing graphics				

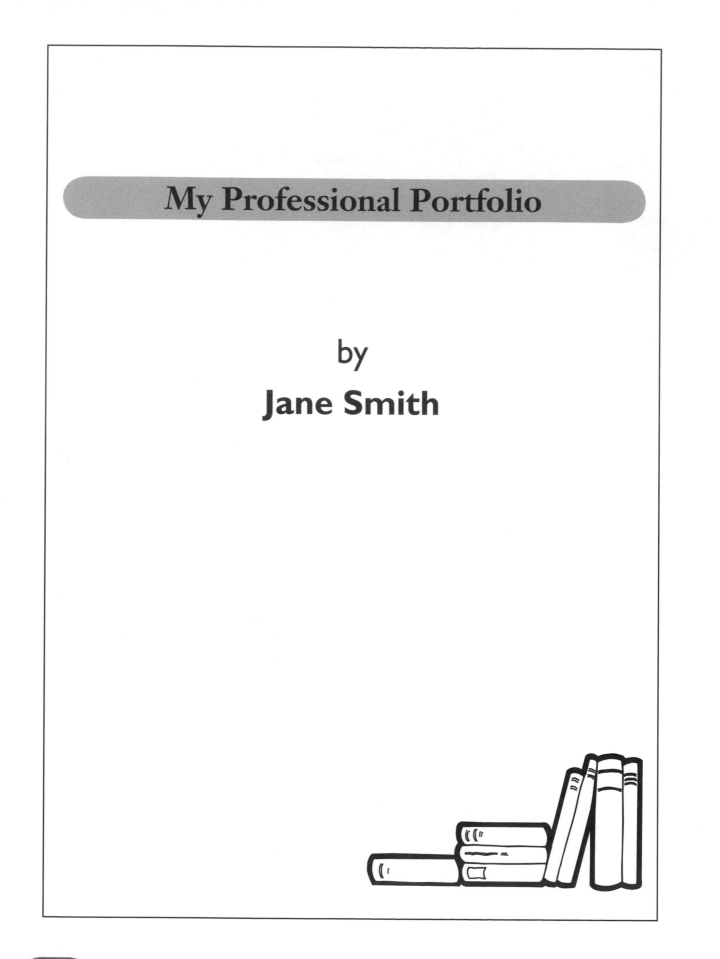

My Professional Portfolio

by

Jane Smith

Table of Contents

- Personal Philosophy

- Professional Goals

- Resume

- Letter of Reference

- Professional Development Plan

- Peter, A Success Story

- Diversity Reflection

- Evaluation

- Technology Reflection

- Sam, A Success Story

- Todd, A Success Story

- Personal Observation

All photographs have been used with appropriate permission granted.

—J. S.

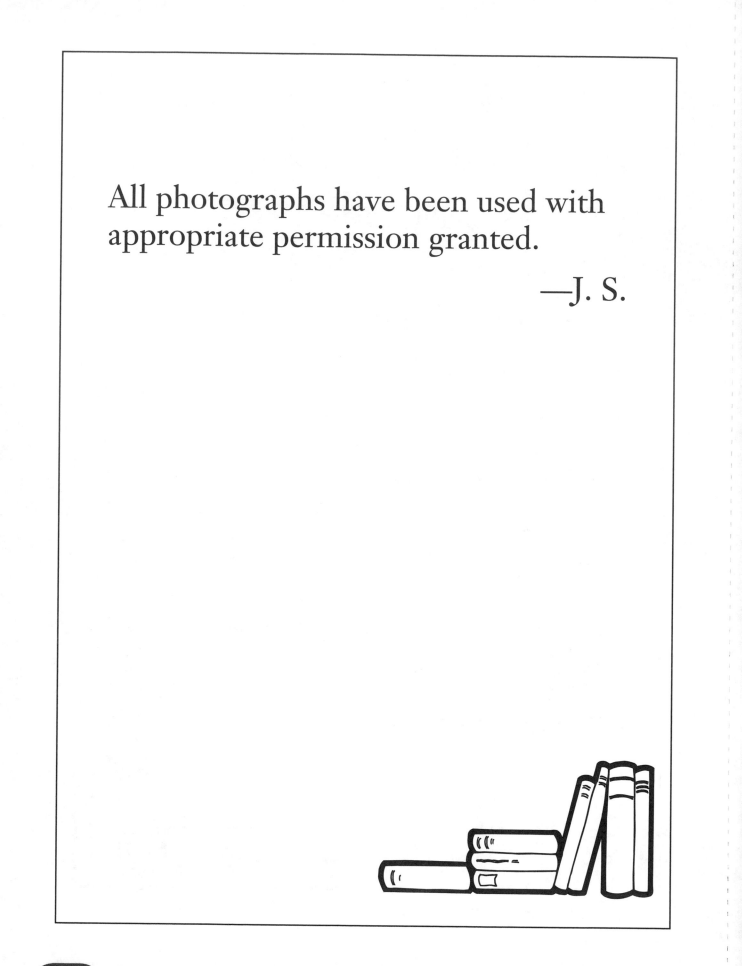

Chapter Nine   How Does One Create an Electronic Portfolio?

Personal Philosophy

I believe the ideal classroom should help students learn and grow to be positive, caring, responsible adults.

My Professional Goals

- I want to do my job in a manner that matches my philosophy

- I want to be a positive, contributing member of the educational team

- I want to continually improve my skills

- I want to explore becoming a teacher someday

Jane Smith
000 Main Street
Milwaukee, WI 53211
(000-222-3434)

Employment Objective
Seeking a paraprofessional position at the elementary school level.

Education

Community College   Instructional Assistant Associate Degree   May 2003 Graduation
Pewaukee, WI   Dean's List, National Honor Society

Experience

(Name) Elementary School   Paraprofessional   August 2003–Present
Milwaukee, WI

Worked cooperatively with a teaching team serving students with multicategorical needs grades one through six. Supported students with significant learning needs and behavioral challenges within the inclusive setting, and worked with small instructional groups to reinforce academic skills. Facilitated communication between special education and general education teachers.

(Name) Elementary School   Paraprofessional   June 2003–August 2003
Milwaukee, WI   Summer Program

Assisted within the districtwide summer school learning disabilities program. Provided daily small group instruction in reading and math using a direct instruction approach. Maintained a daily log of student performance and supervised recreational activities.

Volunteer Activities

Special Olympics Program, (Name) Street School   Coach—After school activity
Community First Program, Milwaukee, WI   Reading Tutor

References and Portfolio

Available upon request

Oak Street Elementary School

WHERE KIDS RULE

March 7, 2004

To Whom It May Concern:

I am principal at Oak Street Elementary School where Jane Smith had her coop experience. I feel qualified to recommend Jane and do so without reservation.

Jane is a person I am always glad to see. She radiates an inner calm and assurance that is uncommon. Jane is a thoughtful person who works hard both in and out of the classroom. While at Oak Street Elementary, she was a valued member of the education team and worked well with students, staff, and parents. Her organizational skills, insights into student behavior, and professionalism are excellent. She sets high standards for herself and is a role model for children and adults.

I am certain Jane Smith will be a positive addition to any district fortunate enough to employ her. I highly recommend her and would be pleased to answer any questions you have regarding her performance while at Oak Street Elementary.

Sincerely,

Douglas Brown
Principal

Professional Development Plan

Goal	Outcome
• To increase sign language skills	• See Peter, A Success Story
• To learn more about diversity	• See Reflection Statement
• To communicate better with teachers	• See Evaluation
• To improve my technology skills	• See Reflection Statement

Peter, A Success Story

Peter has autism and no verbal speech. He used to have tantrums  when he was frustrated. With the supervision of his teacher, I taught him sign language. Now he lets us know by signing when he is frustrated.

Reflection Statement

Knowledge:

To learn more about diversity.

What I did:

I attended a session at the state paraeducator conference on diversity.

What I learned:

I learned a lot! I learned that students from different cultures behave differently than I expected. Sometimes I think they are being disrespectful when actually they are being very polite. I learned that sometimes I am asking them to do things they don't understand and it is just a difference in culture.

How I will use what I learned
or
How I used what I learned:

I will be careful not to misinterpret student behavior. I will try to learn more about the students from different cultures in my class.

Paraprofessional Evaluation

Name: Jane Smith
School(s): Oak Street Elementary
City: Milwaukee, WI
Grade Level(s): Elementary

Place an X over the number from 1–9 to describe the paraprofessional's performance.

CONTINUUM

Excels, 7–9   Performance is above and beyond that which is expected.
Achieved, 4–6   Performance is acceptable but not exceeding that which is expected.
Needs improvement, 1–3   Performance indicates the need for additional time and effort to achieve that which is expected.

THE INSTRUCTIONAL PROCESS

Demonstrates appropriate preparation for classroom instruction.   1 2 3 4 5 6 7 8 **X9**

Reinforces a variety of effective teaching techniques.   1 2 3 4 5 6 7 **X8** 9

Helps provide opportunities for individual differences.   1 2 3 4 5 6 7 8 **X9**

Demonstrates knowledge of subject matter.   1 2 3 4 5 6 7 8 **X9**

Demonstrates the ability to communicate effectively with students.   1 2 3 4 5 6 7 8 **X9**

Demonstrates the ability to communicate effectively with staff.   1 2 3 4 5 6 7 8 **X9**

COMMENTS:

Jane has worked hard to improve her communication skills, especially with staff. She shares information and seeks information from others. Increased communication has led to less confusion and fewer scheduling difficulties.

CLASSROOM MANAGEMENT

Demonstrates ability to appropriately motivate students.   1 2 3 4 5 6 7 **X8** 9

Helps organize classroom environment to promote learning.   1 2 3 4 5 6 7 **X8** 9

Helps manage student behavior in a constructive manner.   1 2 3 4 5 6 7 8 **X9**

COMMENTS:

Behavior management is a strength for Jane. She instinctively analyzes a situation and acts without hesitation. She follows procedures and behavior management plans. She also works to prevent problem behaviors.

Reflection Statement

Topic/Standard/Goal:

To improve my technology skills

What I did:

I created an electronic portfolio. To do this I attended the school technology workshop day, worked with the computer lab assistant every Tuesday after school, worked after school on my own every Wednesday, and reviewed electronic portfolios created by students, teachers, and paraeducators.

What I learned:

I learned how to do the following:
1. *PowerPoint presentations*
2. *Use the digital camera*
3. *Use Photoshop to manipulate photographs*
4. *Insert photographs and images*
5. *Use the scanner*

I also learned how to ask for help and not to be afraid of the computer. Every Tuesday, I had lots of questions to ask the computer lab assistant. I couldn't have done it without her help. Before, I was afraid I would look foolish if I asked a question. I usually tried to do things on my own. I learned that it's okay to try to figure things out on my own but there are times when it's best just to ask. AND I was so afraid of computers. I guess I thought I would break one. But now I am much more comfortable using a computer and know I can learn even more about how to use one.

How I will use what I learned
or
How I used what I learned:

I used what I learned to create this portfolio. The portfolio is done in PowerPoint. I used the digital camera to take a picture of Peter and I inserted the picture into the presentation. I used a scanner for the resume, the reference, the reflections, and the evaluation.

Now I can help students with their technology projects. I can't wait to take more pictures of students. The teacher and I want to try a strategy of "catching them being good" using the digital camera.

Sam, A Success Story

I taught Sam how to use the digital camera. For his Family Assignment,

he took pictures of everyone in his family and made a picture family tree.

Todd, A Success Story

Todd likes to play hockey. He wants to be on the team, but he needs to keep his grades up. I took this digital picture and we taped it to his desk to remind him. Now he has a B average.

> "You gain strength, courage, and confidence by every experience in which you really stop to look fear in the face. You are able to say to yourself, I lived through this horror. I can take the next thing that comes along. . . . You must do the thing you think you cannot do."
>
> —Eleanor Roosevelt, *You Learn by Living* (1960)

I was so afraid of doing this portfolio, especially on the computer! Now I know what it's like "to do the thing you think you cannot do." Eleanor Roosevelt was right. Now I can take the next thing that comes along. I am looking forward to learning new things and improving how I work with students and teachers.

—J. S.

CHAPTER TEN

How Can Supervisors Use the Portfolio for Evaluation?

Administrator Documentation and Evaluation

Paraeducator Highly Qualified Status

Federal legislation now requires a focus on the "highly qualified" status of paraeducators as they perform their role within the school setting. Flexible formats for documenting qualifications have been afforded to states, leading the way to the apropos option of portfolio assessment. Many local school districts across the country have elected to use portfolio assessment as a means of documenting the "highly qualified" status of paraeducators. Rather than struggle with a written test, a portfolio assess-

> We judge ourselves by what we feel capable of doing; others judge us by what we have done.
> — Henry Wadsworth Longfellow

ment and review provides a more explicit and authentic measure of what the paraeducator can do within the classroom.

The Administrator Portfolio Evaluation form (p. 143) can serve as a guide in satisfying official administrative documentation of the skill level of the paraeducator called for under the law. Paraeducators are advised to present the documentation form to the building principal and submit a proposal for a portfolio assessment as an alternative to a written test. From a pragmatic standpoint, the portfolio can give vision and direction to the overall assessment and feedback process. Additionally, employee performance assessment and monitoring is typically conducted on an annual basis within the field of education. Building or district-level administrators usually evaluate teachers, and paraeducators tend to be evaluated by building principals or, in some cases, by the primary teacher with whom they work. For ongoing annual evaluation purposes, again, the portfolio can be used, perhaps paired with an interview or an on-site, classroom observation.

The paraeducator is encouraged to self-advocate and build a case for a portfolio evaluation format. Collaborate with other paraeducators and perhaps produce a prototype portfolio and pursue the benefits of a meaningful evaluation process. The role of the paraeducator can be complex and the portfolio allows a differentiated evaluation process to address the complexity of the job.

ADMINISTRATOR PORTFOLIO EVALUATION

Documentation of Qualified Paraeducator

Paraeducator's Name: _____ Date Portfolio Submitted: _____

Position Held: _____ School Employed: _____

Dates of Employment: from _____ to _____ Supervising Teacher: _____

Date of Portfolio Review: _____
Reviewed by: _____ Title: _____

Portfolio Documents Reviewed
_____ Resume
_____ Letters of Reference
_____ Evidence of Qualification

Subject	Applicable Grade Level	Artifact Description	Reflective/Descriptive Summary
READING			
WRITING			
MATH			
Other			

_____ Evidence of Training
_____ Goal Statements

Determination of Review
_____ Documents and portfolio review indicate paraeducator is highly qualified.
_____ Documents and portfolio review indicate paraeducator is **NOT** highly qualified.

Administrator signature: _____ Date: _____

Paraeducator Training Program Portfolio Evaluation

As a capstone assessment feature, a program portfolio can be used to document skills and knowledge acquired through formal training within a higher educational institution. Artifacts selected by the student or required through coursework may vary significantly from one institution to another and typically relate to particular courses and artifacts created within those courses. Completed work samples and philosophy statements should be revised and adjusted based on instructor feedback before including such in the portfolio. Program portfolios generally combine self-selection and required components. Due to the complexity of the portfolio assessment process, a pass/fail review format is a viable grading option.

Use of the comprehensive portfolio checklist discussed earlier in this manual can offer structure in grading as required items are highlighted and checked off. An additional form (Paraeducator Program—Portfolio Evaluation) follows for use in identifying course specific artifacts or documents for inclusion in the program portfolio.

> Challenges make you discover things about yourself that you never really knew.
>
> —Cicely Tyson